CLASSICAL COMPOSERS

Florence PRICE

by Joanne Mattern
with Consultation by John Viscardi,
Executive Director of Classic Lyric Arts
illustrated by Marilena Perilli

RED CHAIR PRESS
Egremont, Massachusetts

Classical Composers has been produced and published by Red Chair Press Books for Young Readers:
Red Chair Press LLC PO Box 333 South Egremont, MA 01258
www.redchairpress.com

Download a Free Activity Guide on our website.

For more information about Classic Lyric Arts, visit www.classiclyricarts.org.

Names: Mattern, Joanne, 1963- author. | Viscardi, John, consultant. | Perilli, Marilena, illustrator.

Title: Florence Price / by Joanne Mattern, with consultation by John Viscardi, executive director of Classic Lyric Arts ; illustrated by Marilena Perilli.

Description: Egremont, Massachusetts : Red Chair Press, [2025] | Series: Classical composers | Interest age level: 007-010. | Includes bibliographical references and index. | Summary: Florence Price (1887–1953), an American composer and pianist, was a trailblazer as the first African-American woman to gain recognition in classical music ... Colorful illustrations plus photographs of meaningful sites and settings connect readers to important points in Price's history. A timeline and B Sharp sidebars add details to the composer's life story.--Publisher.

Identifiers: ISBN: 978-1-64371-448-6 (LB hardcover) | 978-1-64371-449-3 (paperback) | 978-1-64371-451-6 (S&L ebook) | LCCN: 2024936091

Subjects: LCSH: Price, Florence, 1887-1953--Juvenile literature. | Women composers--United States-- Biography--Juvenile literature. | African American composers--Biography--Juvenile literature. | CYAC: Price, Florence, 1887-1953. | Composers--United States--Biography. | LCGFT: Biographies. | BISAC: JUVENILE NONFICTION / Biography & Autobiography / Music. | JUVENILE NONFICTION / Biography & Autobiography / Performing Arts. | JUVENILE NONFICTION / Music / Classical. | JUVENILE NONFICTION / Biography & Autobiography / Women.

Classification: LCC: ML410.P835 M38 2025 | DDC: 780.92--dc23

Image credits: p.4 Portrait of Florence Price: University of Arkansas Libraries, Fayetteville, MC 988, Box 1, Folder 12, Item 1; p.16 Florence Price: University of Arkansas Libraries, Fayetteville, MC 988a, Series 1, Box 2, Folder 1, Item 3; p.25 Photograph of Florence Price and Florence Price Robinson Looking at Flowers in an Outdoor Garden: University of Arkansas Libraries, Fayetteville, MC 988a, Box 2, Folder 2; p.26 Portrait of Florence Price Seated at a Piano: University of Arkansas Libraries, Fayetteville, MC 988a, Box 2, Folder 2, Item 1; p.28 Performance of Florence Price's music: University of Arkansas Libraries, Fayetteville, ML/3556/P38/1968; p. 31 Portrait of Florence Price at a Side Angle from About 1933: University of Arkansas Libraries, Fayetteville, MC 988a, Box 2, Folder 1, Item 3; pp. 6, 13, 20 Library of Congress

Illustrations: Marilena Perilli, except p. 7 by Joe LeMonnier

Printed in the United States of America

0425 1P CGF25

Table of Contents

A Blessed Childhood 4

Florence at School 10

A Big Move 16

A Great Honor 20

Treasure in an Old House 24

Florence Rediscovered 26

Timeline 30

Glossary 32

Read More 32

Index 32

A Blessed Childhood

It wasn't easy to be a woman composer during the 1900s. It was even harder to succeed if you were Black. Florence Price defied these odds. She was a popular composer during her life. Then a surprising discovery brought her back to popularity long after her death.

Florence Smith was born in Little Rock, Arkansas, on April 9, 1887. Her father, James, was the only Black dentist in Little Rock. Her mother, who was also named Florence, had been a music teacher before she married. Later, she ran a restaurant and worked as a secretary in a bank.

Main Street Little Rock, Arkansas around 1900.

B# **B SHARP:** Florence's family was wealthy. She grew up in a beautiful home filled with books where she learned to play on her family's grand piano.

ILLINOIS
KANSAS
MISSOURI
ARKANSAS
TENNESSEE
OKLAHOMA
Little Rock
MISSISSIPPI
LOUISIANA
TEXAS

Florence's mother taught her to play the piano when Florence was very young. When she was just four years old, Florence performed in public for the first time. She played in a **recital** with other young musicians.

When Florence was 11 years old, she published her first **composition**. She would continue to write music for the rest of her life.

At one time, she wrote a new piece of music using both classical style combined with music from the Black **spiritual** "Sinner Don't Let This Harvest Pass." It was a big hit when first performed.

Florence at School

Florence was very good at school. She did well with all her subjects. Florence was so smart she skipped several grades. At that time, Black students and white students went to separate schools. School buildings for Blacks were often falling apart. And students had to learn from old textbooks that had been thrown out from the white-only schools.

Florence did not let her school's poor conditions stop her from learning. At Union High School, she studied Greek, Latin, history, science, and many other advanced subjects. She graduated from high school when she was just 14 years old.

B# **B SHARP:** Florence graduated at the top of her high school class.

Even though Florence was only 14 when she graduated, she wanted to go to college. Her parents thought she could get a better education in the northern United States. Schools in the North were not **segregated**.

Florence was accepted at the New England Conservatory of Music in Boston, Massachusetts. She studied organ and piano. Florence also studied music composition. One of her teachers was George Whitefield Chadwick. Chadwick was interested in spirituals and other traditional Black music.

The New England Conservatory in Boston, shown as Price would have seen it.

B#

B SHARP: Florence lied and told the New England Conservatory that she was Mexican to avoid poor treatment because she was Black.

After she graduated from the New England Conservatory, Florence moved back home to Arkansas. She worked as a music teacher for a few years.

Florence did not stay in Little Rock for long. In 1910, she moved to Atlanta, Georgia. She got a job as head of the music department at Clark Atlanta University. Then, in 1912, Florence married a lawyer named Thomas J. Price. The two of them moved back to Little Rock.

B#

B SHARP: Price performed at her college graduation. This was a great **honor**. Only nine students out of the 50 graduates were chosen to perform.

A Big Move

The Prices had three children. Life in Little Rock was good for a while. However, there was a lot of violence toward Black people. In 1927, the family moved to Chicago. Many other Black families moved north at that time. This movement was called the Great Migration.

Price went back to school in Chicago. She studied music. She also studied foreign languages and English. Price loved to learn!

In 1931, Price and her husband divorced. Price had to work to support herself and her children. For a while, she played the piano at silent movies. She also composed music for radio advertisements.

To save money, Price and her daughters moved in with her friend, Margaret Bonds. Many famous Black artists visited the Bonds. It was here that Price met the famous writer Langston Hughes. She also met a well-known singer named Marian Anderson. Later, Hughes, Anderson, and Price would work together.

Langston Hughes

Marian Anderson

A Great Honor

In 1932, Price entered a contest for Black composers. She won! Price won a $500 first prize for her ***Symphony*** *Number 1*. She also won a $250 prize for a piano **sonata**.

Price was happy to win the money. But an even bigger prize was in store for her. In 1933, Price's *Symphony Number 1* was performed by the Chicago Symphony **Orchestra**. It was the first composition by a Black woman to be performed by a major American orchestra.

NEWS
SYMPHONY NUMBER
TO BE PERFORMED BY
CHICAGO
SYMPHONY ORCHESTRA

Soon other orchestras began performing Price's works. She wrote hundreds of compositions. Some were symphonies. Others were works for piano, organ, or violin. Price also wrote chamber music. This type of music is performed by a small group of musicians.

Price is celebrated for writing beautiful classical music. But she also used music from the black churches she heard all around her. This idea of combining classical style with modern influences continues today in classical symphony and opera.

In 1940, Price was **inducted** into the American Society of Composers, Authors, and Publishers. Her induction honored her work as a groundbreaking **composer**.

Treasure in an Old House

Florence Price died on June 3, 1953. Orchestras no longer performed her music. Soon, Price's work was forgotten. Then, something amazing happened.

Price had a summer home in St. Anne, Illinois. Over the years, the house was abandoned and robbed. In 2009, Vicki and Darrell Gatwood bought the house. They found sheet music scattered all over the floor. The music had been written by Florence Price.

Florence Price shown here with her oldest daughter, Florence Louise Robinson in the garden at the St. Anne house.

Florence Rediscovered

The Gatwoods donated Price's music to the University of Arkansas. Many people were interested in this great discovery. Orchestras began performing her work again. In 2018, a major music publisher announced that it would publish her newly found work. People are able to rediscover Price's music all over again, 65 years after her death.

Violin Concerto No. 2 was one of the pieces that was thought to be lost.

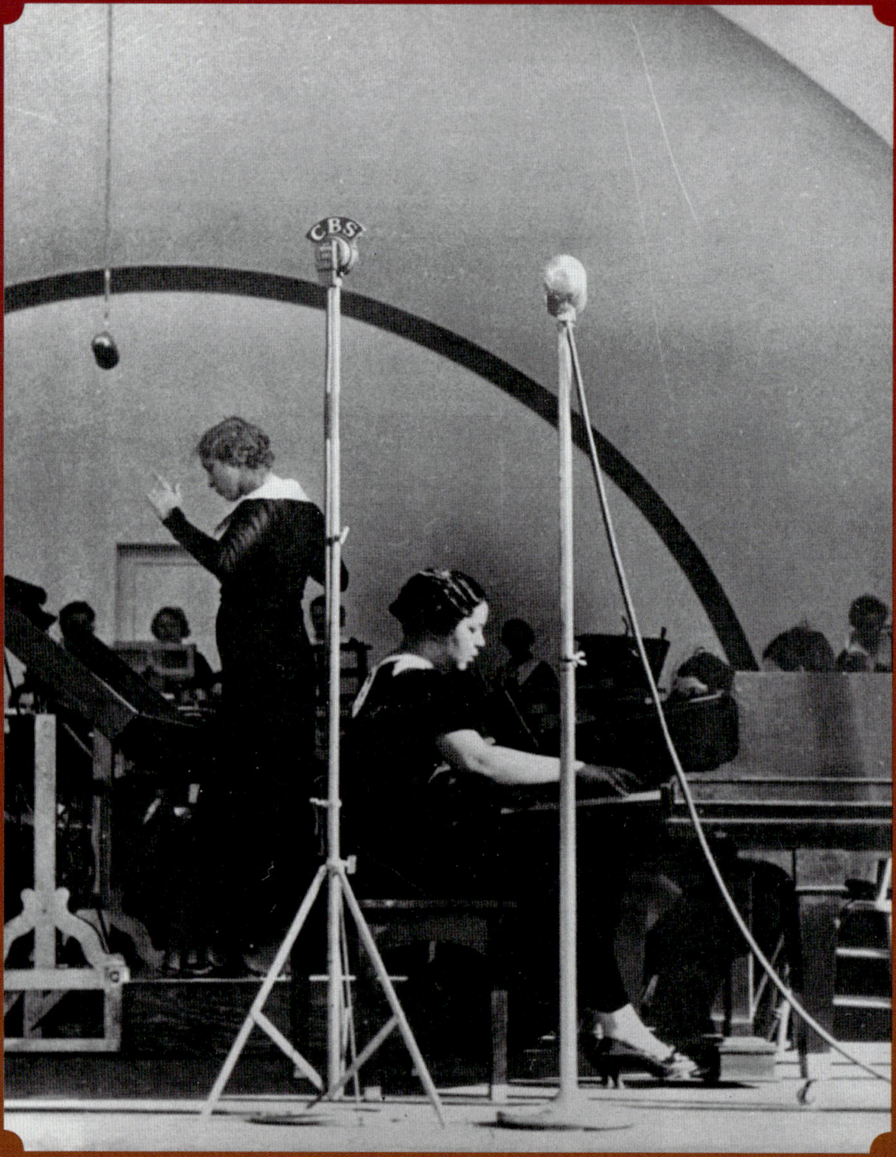

Price's Piano Concerto in One Movement was first played in public by her friend Marilyn Bonds (at piano) and the Women's Symphony Orchestra of Chicago at the 1933 Chicago World's Fair.

Florence Price had been trained as a classical pianist. But traditional Black music was also an important part of her life. She combined these two traditions to create a kind of classical music that was different from anything else.

Price knew that she faced a difficult road as a Black woman composer. She once wrote, "I have two handicaps—those of sex and race." Despite the prejudice of the times, Price was able to create beautiful music. She is remembered today as a **pioneer** in classical music.

B# **B SHARP:** Price often used spirituals and traditional Black music in her works. One of her most famous songs was, "I Am Bound for the Kingdom."

Important Dates in Florence Price's Life

1887	Florence Smith is born in Little Rock, Arkansas.
1891	Smith gives her first public performance at 4 years old.
1910	At age 14, Smith graduates from the New England Conservatory of Music.
1912	Smith marries Thomas Price.
1927	The Price family moves to Chicago.
1931	Price and her husband divorce.
1933	Price's *Symphony No. 1* is performed for the first time by the Chicago Symphony Orchestra.
1953	Price dies on June 3 in Chicago.
2009	Price's work is rediscovered in an abandoned house.
2018	Florence Price's lost compositions are published for the first time.

Portrait of Florence Price from 1933.

Glossary

composer a person who writes music

composition a written work

defied refused to obey

honor great respect

inducted to become a member of an organization

orchestra a large group of musicians who play music together on different instruments

pioneer the first to do something

recital a performance by a person or a small group

segregated separated by race

sonata a piece of music for a solo instrument, sometimes with piano playing as well

spirituals music most closely related to the Black African slaves in the American South

symphony a long piece of music written for an orchestra

Read More About Price

Kaufman Music Center. *Who is Florence Price?* New York: Schirmer Trade Books, 2021.

Index

American Society of Composers 23
Anderson, Marian. 19
Arkansas, Little Rock. . . 6, 15, 16
Arkansas, University of 26
Atlanta 15
Bonds, Margaret 19
Boston 12, 13
Chadwick, George Whitefield 12
Chicago. 16
Chicago Symphony Orchestra. 20
Clark Atlanta University 15
Great Migration. 16
Hughes, Langston 19
Illinois, St. Anne 24
New England Conservatory 12–13, 15
Price, Thomas J. 15